Koala's Book of Poems
by
Esta de Fossard

Illustrations by Rosemary Wilson
Photographs by Neil McLeod

The Koala Stories · Series 3

Published by

Edward Arnold (Australia) Pty. Ltd.

For Gordon and Gotch Limited

KANGA'S JOEY

Has anybody seen Kanga's Joey?
He ran away and didn't tell his Mum.
She said she'd let him know
When it was time to go,
But when she called, he simply didn't come.

Has anybody seen Kanga's Joey?
Hey, Possum, is he hiding there with you?
Has he fallen on his face
In a very muddy place?
Or has he run away to find a zoo?

Has anybody seen Kanga's Joey?
Emu — can you see him if you stretch your neck up high?
Can you see inside that nest,
Did he crawl in there to rest?
Or to ask the birds to teach him how to fly?

Hasn't *anybody* seen Kanga's Joey?
Doesn't *anybody* know where he would go?
Oh look, he's coming — there!
Now tell us, Joey, where . . .
Where were you, Joey? Just where did you go?

POUCHES

"I've got a pouch," says Kangaroo,
"And Wallaby has one, too —
And so have Koala and Possum and Wombat.
We've all got pouches — have you?"

"If you don't have a pouch, then what do you do
With your toys, your tissue, your snack?
If you don't have a pouch to put things in,
Do you carry them around on your back?"

"Or perhaps you've a pocket, a pocket or two.
Yes a pocket could do, I s'pose.
But could it hold a tummy, four paws and a tail,
Two eyes, two ears and a nose?"

EMU BALLET

Brolga dances a graceful dance
And Possum watches and sighs,
"I wish I could dance the way Brolga does!"
"It's easy," Emu replies.

Brolga stretches her soft grey wings
And dances with beauty and grace.
Emu tries to copy the steps,
And falls flat on his emu face!

Brolga stands on one leg and bows
And arches her neck to the sky.
Emu — boastfully — does the same thing,
And falls flat on his emu eye!

Brolga glides upwards and forwards and flies,
And moves on with beauty and ease.
Emu jumps high in an effort to fly,
And lands CRASH on his emu knees!

"Oh Emu," says Possum, "How silly you are!
Why try to be something you're not!"
"I can be what I choose," screams Emu and leaps —
To land FLOP on his big Emu bott!

WHAT EMU KNOWS

If you knew
what Emu knew,
you'd know you knew
a thing or two.

You'd know
no emu ever flew,
or ever grew
to be a gnu!
Or dressed itself
in green and blue;
or ate a pot
of gumboot stew.

If you knew
what Emu knew
you'd know you knew
the things you knew.

You'd know you hated
emu 'flu
and noisy dogs
that hassle you,
and rides on a bus
to Woolloomooloo
and sandwiches made
of chocolate and glue!

If you knew
what Emu knew,
you'd know you knew
what suited you.

You'd know what Emu
would like to do —
To ride on a bicycle
built for two;
and eat peanut brittle
in a gold canoe;
To visit the king
of ancient Peru,
And say to that king,
"I'm smarter than you!"

That's what Emu
would like to do!
How about you?

REFLECTIONS ON A REFLECTION

When I look down
What do I see?
Do I see you?
Or do I see me?
Am I me?
Or am I you?
It's hard to know
Just who is who.
Are you you?
Or are you me?
I'm not quite sure
Who I should be.
Am I one?
Or are we two?
Which one is me?
And which is you?
Are we me?
Or am I we?
I wish I knew
Which us is we.
It's all too much;
It's not quite fair.
In fact, I think
I just don't care.
I think I'll go —
But I wish I knew —
Is it me that's going,
Or is it you?

IMAGINE IF . . .

Imagine if
Koala had a crest like a white cockatoo,
And Wombat had legs like a deer,
And Rabbit had a tail as long as a cow's —
Now wouldn't that seem very queer!

Imagine if
Emu liked to live in a tree in a nest,
And Rosella had wings made of string,
And Possum could neigh like a very big horse —
Now wouldn't that be a strange thing!

Imagine if
Kangaroo had ears like an elephant's ears,
And Platypus flew like a bird,
And Goanna grew wool like a soft, fleecy sheep,
Now wouldn't that just be absurd!

So, perhaps, in the end, it's all just as well
That things look the way that they do.
At least, as it is, we can tell what is what,
And know, at a glance, who is who.

THE WORLD OF BACKWARDS

Koala sat in his tree one day
And gazed in a looking glass,
And as he stared at that mirrored world
The oddest of things came to pass.
Everything turned itself front to back,
And appeared the opposite way.
So the animals there by Koala's big tree
All looked quite backwards that day.

There, on his long legs, ran **Ume**
With his tall neck stretched up high,
While **Ootakcoc** sat on his favourite perch
And raised a crest to the sky.
There through the branches, red **Allesor** flew
And called to shy **Mussop** below,
While scuffling around in the side of the hill
Looking for roots, was **Tabmow**!
And sure enough, in a sunny spot
Lay **Annaog** sleeping all day,
While **Arrubakook** laughed from the branches above
To see **Ooragnak** hopping away!

Koala turned round to look at his friends,
Without that strange mirror between,
And said, "The way that you are is much better by far
Than that weird backwards way you have been!"

FIVE THINGS THAT ARE . . . PERHAPS

Hey — what's that noise I heard?
I think my boomer-rang!
Please throw it away,
It's too noisy — HEY!
It's after me! Stop it! Help! "BANG".

Good grief — my didgerididn't!
Now what shall I do?
If a didgeridon't,
Or a didgeriwon't —
How do you make a didgeri*doo*?

Look at that little dingo,
The one in the floppy hat.
He wants to play cricket,
He's in front of the wicket —
But he's forgotten to bring his dingbat!

If rocks make a waterfall fall —
Then what makes a billabong bong?
Is it just 'cos of some
Burpy gas in its tum,
Or is that really a billabong song?

Just look at that kangaroo!
He's not acting like he usedta!
He rises at dawn,
And crows on the lawn.
Does he think he's a kangarooster?

WHAT CAN A BILLYCAN DO?

What can a billycan do for you?
What can a billycan do?
A billycan can do
Many, many things for you;
That's what a billycan can do
For you!

A billycan can carry things, carry things, carry things;
A billycan can carry things, for you.
Things like —
Rocks and socks, and eggs and pegs,
And jam and ham, and rings and strings,
And slugs and mugs, and rice and spice,
And brushes and thrushes, and cherries and berries,
And trumpets and crumpets, and papers and capers,
And candlesticks and building bricks,
And sunflower seeds and coloured beads,
And nice cool drinks and tiddleywinks,
AND
lots and lots and lots and lots of small, tender,
  green gum leaf tips
that taste better than anything else in the whole
  wide world!

QUOKKA

If Quokka chose a time for bed
Would ten o'quock appeal?
And if Quokka joined the orchestra
Would he play the Quokkenspiel?
If Quokka had a rooster
Would it say Quok-a-doodle-do?
And if Quokka brought a friend to play,
Would it be a Quokka-too?

IF I COULD FLY AWAY

If I could fly away like Cockatoo
You wouldn't find me sitting in a tree.
I wouldn't sit and chew
Like other koalas do,
I'd fly away to see what I could see.

I'd fly off to Chile
Carrying my billy
And I'd get a load of coffee beans for free.
Then I'd go to Wales for weeks
To find some fresh Welsh leeks
That I could give to Rabbit for his tea.
Then off I'd fly again
To land in sunny Spain
To get a Spanish onion or two.
Then perhaps I'd go to Chad
Or drop in on Baghdad
To find a shiny something for Emu.

Just think of all the things
I could see if I had wings.
But I don't, so there's nothing I can do —
But sit here in my tree
And imagine where I'd be
If I could fly away like Cockatoo.

MUD

Mud, mud, mud,
Makes a wonderful platypus pud-
dle,
With ooze, ooze, ooze,
The sort that a platypus choos-
es
Where there're yabbies and wormies and fish
To fulfil happy platypus wish-
es.
Nothing else in the world gives such glee
To a duck-billed, web-footed platy-
pus,
As mud, mud, mud!

KOALA'S ADVICE
TO THOSE WHO HEAR A BUNYIP
IN THE MIDDLE OF THE NIGHT

When you're sleeping in your gum tree
In the middle of the night,
And you hear a scrubbly stomping
That wakes you up in fright,
And you know that all that scrubbling
And that somewhat gurbly growl
Is a mean old Big Bad Bunyip Beast
Going somewhere on the prowl,
And you know that when that Bunyip
Starts to snorble in its nose,
You'd be safer to be anywhere
Than where that Bunyip goes —
THEN . . .
You'd better close your eyes up tight
And curl yourself up small,
And try to lie completely still
And make no sound at all,
And hope that if you're lucky
And there's no moon in the sky,
Then that mean old Big Bad Bunyip Beast
Will go scrubbling right on by!

MENU FOR A BUNYIP

What does a Bunyip like eating for tea?
I'll bet you could just never guess.
He's quite fond of noses, and green pickled toeses
Mashed up in a globulous mess!
He adores porridge lumps, and old rubbish dumps,
And slime served with long stringy goo —
But what he likes most on green mouldy toast,
With dish water gravy is — YOU.

KOALA'S ADVICE
TO THOSE WHO FEEL FRIGHTENED,
SHY OR LONELY

When your heart says, "I'm frightened",
And your eyes start to cry.
When your tummy feels all squibbly,
And your voice says, "Oh, my!"
When your skin goes all bumpy
And you want to run away,
Then it's time to take yourself in hand
And say, "Hey, self, hey!"
Stand tall, breathe deep, count up to ten!
Shout loudly, "I'm not scared".
And you'll soon feel brave again.

When you're standing in a corner
And you're feeling VERY shy;
And no-one seems to see you,
And you want to say, "Bye-bye";
When you're sure you're looking foolish,
And you're feeling like a flop;
It's time to shake yourself down hard,
And say "Stop, self. *Stop*!"
Stand tall, smile wide, say, "How do you do?"
Tell the world, "I'm me, world",
And the shys won't bother you.

When you're feeling VERY lonely,
And there's no-one there to play.
When all your games are boring,
And it's a stinky, horrid day.
When you're sure that no-one loves you.
And you wish that you were dead,
It's time to turn yourself around
And say, "Self, be a friend instead".
Think big, think hard; someone needs a friend for sure.
Make a phone call, send a letter —
You won't be lonely any more.

The Publisher, Author and Photographer acknowledge with thanks the facilities and assistance provided by the Sir Colin MacKenzie Fauna Park, Healesville, Victoria.

© Esta de Fossard 1984
First published 1984 by
Edward Arnold (Australia) Pty Ltd
80 Waverley Road
Caulfield East, Victoria 3145

Edward Arnold (Publishers) Ltd
41 Bedford Square
London WC1B 3DQ

300 North Charles Street
Baltimore MD 21201 USA

National Library of Australia
Cataloguing-in-publication data
De Fossard, Esta, 1934–
   Koala's book of poems.
   For children.
   ISBN 0 7131 8101 X
   ISBN 0 7131 8102 8 (kit of book and cassette)
   1. Children's poetry, Australian. I. McLeod,
Neil. II. Wilson, Rosemary. III. Title.
A821'.3

Photography: Neil McLeod
Drawings: Rosemary Wilson
Book Design: Stott & Twelftree, Melbourne
Set in Garamond by Meredith Trade Lino Pty
Ltd, Melbourne
Printed by Tien Wah Press